Richard L. MacDonnelll

Dissecting Room Record

Richard L. MacDonnelll

Dissecting Room Record

ISBN/EAN: 9783337377755

Printed in Europe, USA, Canada, Australia, Japan

Cover: Foto ©Thomas Meinert / pixelio.de

More available books at **www.hansebooks.com**

MEDICAL FACULTY

M^cGILL COLLEGE

DISSECTING ROOM RECORD

Roll of the Practical Anatomy Class
for 1887 – 1888.

1. Addy
2. Alexander D.
3. Anderson
4 Anet
5. Aylen
6. Burritt
7 Bissett
8 Busby
9 Brown
10 Browse
11 Bowie
12 Beers
13 Broderick
14 Bowes
15 Beaman
16. Bennie
17. Blanchard
Clemesha
Clark
Curtis
Calkin E
Calkin W.

Conolly
Corbin
Clune
Carlaw
Clark J.
Coleman
Douglas
Erwar
Evans
Esson
Ellis
Farwell
Fulton
Fletcher
Forrell
Graftin
Green
Hayes
Harrison
Holton
Hilton
Hattie
Hartin
Hamilton hv
Hamilton WJ.

Hughes Mr.	Murphy
Hall	McEwan
Harris	McDonald Mr.
Hickey	McLennan A.
Luksetter	McKee
Internoscia	McKechnie
Lento	McGuire
Jenkins	McPhail
Kemp	McCrimmon
Kerr	McDonald A.
Kyle	McGauran
Kelley	McManus
Keir	McCann
Kent	McMillan
Kee	McEown
Lucas	McLean D.N.
Lewin	McKenzie
Liddell	
Lambert	Noble
Louring	Neil
Moore	O'Connor
Mulligan	Oliver
Martin	Patton
Murray	Parke G.H.
Morris	Ross J
Mader	Robertson
Moss	R Robertson J.J.
Main	Robertson E.A
Morrow	
Mutch	

Reid
Richards
Ross HR
Reed.
Smith WD
Spier
Smith A G
Smith I H.
Saphir
Sharling.
Ivory
Tunstall
Telfer
Thompson FL.
Lackaberry.
Weeks
Wheeler
Whyte
Williamson
Webster
Woodruffe
Wood
Wilson
Williamson
Watson
Yorston.

This record was begun at the date of
the passing of the Amended Anatomy Act. which
was also the date of my appointment as Demonstrator
of Anatomy. April. 1883.

R L Macdonnell.

Name *Lizzie Burns*

Received *April 13th 1883* 188 *from* Montreal General Hospital

Sex *Female* Religion *Rome* Cause of Death *Interstitial nephritis*

Buried in the *Roman Catholic* Cemetery on

the *Feb 8th* 1884 . *Age 40 -*

REMARKS:

Name *Jonathan Hindle*

Received *April 20th* 1886 *from* Montreal General Hospital

Sex *Male* Religion *Ch of England* Cause of Death *Chronic Nephritis*

Buried in the *Mount Royal* Cemetery on

the *12th December* 188

REMARKS:

Name *Henry Johnson*

Received *May 25th* 188 *from* Montreal General Hospital

Sex *Male* Religion *Ch of England* Cause of Death *Acute Enteritis*

Buried in the *Mount Royal Cemetery* Cemetery on

the *8th November* 1883 .

REMARKS:

1

Name Honoré Pontbriant   **2**

     Received June 16th 1883 ⋈ *from* Montreal General Hospital

Sex male *Religion* Rome *Cause of Death* Phthisis

Buried in the Roman Catholic   *Cemetery on*

the Dec 12th   1883 .

REMARKS:

Name Martin McKimont

     Received June 28th 1883 *from* Montreal General Hospital

Sex Male *Religion* Presbyterian *Cause of Death* Phthisis

Buried in the Mount Royal Cem   *Cemetery on*

the   188

REMARKS:

Name Eliza Heaton

     Received July 6th 1883 *from* Montreal General Hospital.

Sex Female *Religion* Ch of England *Cause of Death* Phthisis

Buried in the Mount Royal   *Cemetery on*

the   188

REMARKS:

Name   Henry Gall

Received July 31 st 1883 from Montreal General Hospital

Sex Male Religion Ch of England Cause of Death Heart disease.

Buried in the Mount Royal   Cemetery on

the 12th December . 1883

REMARKS:

An old soldier.

Name   Regina Dupuis

Received August 2nd 1883 from Hotel Dieu

Sex Female Religion Rome Cause of Death

Buried in the Roman Catholic   Cemetery on

the 8th February 1884

REMARKS:

Name   Georgina Bilodeau

Received Sept 5th 1883 from Montreal General Hospital

Sex Female Religion Rome Cause of Death Typhoid fever

Buried in the Roman Catholic   Cemetery on

the 8th February 1884 .

REMARKS:

Name *Margaret Wickham* **4**

Received *Sept 7th* 188 **3** from *Montreal General Hospital*

Sex *Female* Religion *Rome* Cause of Death *Chronic dysentery*

Buried in the *Roman Catholic* Cemetery on

the *8th February* 188 **4**

REMARKS:

Name *John Worsley*

Received *Sept 8th* 188 **3** from *Montreal General Hospital*

Sex *Male* Religion *Ch of England* Cause of Death *Typhoid fever*

Buried in the *Roman Mount Royal* ———— Cemetery on

the *12th December* 188 **3** .

REMARKS:

Name *Francis Lafleur*

Received *Sept 10th* 188 **3** from *Hotel Dieu*.

Sex *Male* Religion *Rome* Cause of Death *Evidently dropsy*

Buried in the *Roman Catholic* Cemetery on

the *12th December* 188 **3** .

REMARKS:

Name *Basile Proulx*   5

    Received *Sept 12th* 188 3 *from* Longue Pointe Asylum

Sex *Male* Religion *Rome* *Cause of Death*

Buried in the *Roman Catholic* Cemetery on

the *8th February 12th Dec* 188 43.

REMARKS:

Name *Narcisse Plantin alias Marie Thibeault*

    Received *Sept 13th* 188 3 *from* Notre Dame Hospital

Sex *Female* Religion *Rome* *Cause of Death*

Buried in the *Roman Catholic*. Cemetery on

the *8th February* 188 4

REMARKS:

Name *Urbain Chatelain*

    Received *Sept 25th* 188 3 *from* Notre Dame Hospital

Sex *Male* Religion *Rome* *Cause of Death* Railroad injury

Buried in the *Roman Catholic* Cemetery on

the *8th February* 188 4

REMARKS:

Name Joshua Lees
     Received Sept 28th 1883 from Montreal General Hospital
Sex Male Religion Ch of England Cause of Death Phthisis
Buried in the Mount Royal ———————— Cemetery on
the 12th December 1883.

REMARKS:

Name James Hone
     Received Oct 2rd 1883 from the Coroner
Sex Male Religion Rome Cause of Death Accident.
Buried in the Roman Catholic ——————— Cemetery on
the 12th December 1883.

REMARKS:
A sailor, met with his death by falling down a hatchway.

Name Annie Leonard
     Received 16th March 1883 from Montreal General Hospital
Sex Female Religion Rome Cause of Death
Buried in the Roman Catholic Cemetery on
the 188

REMARKS:

Name *Andrew McCarthy*

   Received *Oct 3rd* 188 **3** *from* *Montreal General Hospital*

Sex *Male* Religion *Rome* Cause of Death

Buried in the *Roman Catholic* Cemetery on

the *12th December* 188 **3** .

REMARKS:

Name *Charles Thibeaudeau*

   Received *12th October* 188 **3** *from* *the Greys Nuns*

Sex *Male* Religion *Rome* Cause of Death

Buried in the *Roman Catholic* Cemetery on

the *8th February* 188 **4**

REMARKS:

Name *Brigette Lajoie*

   Received *October 18th* 188 **3** *from* *Mayer Pointe Asylum*

Sex *Female* Religion *Rome* Cause of Death

Buried in the *Roman Catholic* Cemetery on

the *8th February* 188 **4** .

REMARKS:

Name

Received ~~Sorel~~ Oct 27th 188 3 from Sorel

Sex *Male* Religion *Rome* Cause of Death

Buried in the *Roman Catholic* Cemetery on

the 188

REMARKS:

Name *John Barnes*

Received *Oct 30th* 188 3 from *Montreal Gaol*

Sex *Male* Religion *Rome* Cause of Death

Buried in the *Roman Catholic* Cemetery on

the 188

REMARKS:

Name *Mary Williams*
    Received *31st October* 1883 *from Asile de la Providence*
Sex *Female* Religion *Rome* Cause of Death
Buried in the *Roman Catholic* Cemetery on
the *8th February* 1884.
REMARKS:

Name *Therese Aubin*
    Received *December 5th* 1886 *from Montreal General Hospital*
Sex *Female* Religion *Rome* Cause of Death
Buried in the *Roman Catholic* Cemetery on
the *8th February*. 1884.
REMARKS:

Name *Marie Hudon*
    Received *December 7th* 1883 *from Hospice St Charles*
Sex *Female* Religion *Rome* Cause of Death
Buried in the *Roman Catholic* Cemetery on
the *8th February* 1884
REMARKS:

Name *Michael Ward*
  Received *December 8th 1883* from *Montreal General Hospital*
Sex *Male* Religion *Rome* Cause of Death
Buried in the *Roman Catholic*   Cemetery on
the   188

REMARKS:

Name *Marie Patenaude*
  Received *October 10th 1883* from *Longue Pointe Asylum*
Sex *Female* Religion *Rome* Cause of Death
Buried in the *Roman Catholic*   Cemetery on
the   188

REMARKS:

Name *Henrietta Beauvier*
  Received *Dec 11th* 1883 from
Sex *Female* Religion *Rome* Cause of Death
Buried in the *Roman Catholic*   Cemetery on
the   188

REMARKS:

Name *Damase Michaud*   11

    Received *19ᵗʰ December* 1883 *from* *Longue Pointe Asylum*

Sex *Male* Religion *Rome* *Cause of Death* .

Buried in the *Roman Catholic*   Cemetery on

the   *March 28ᵗʰ*   1884 .

REMARKS:

Name *Jean B Mallette*

    Received *January 21ˢᵗ* 1884 *from* *Hospice St Charles.*

Sex *Male* Religion *Rome* *Cause of Death*

Buried in the *R* :   Cemetery on

the   188

REMARKS:

Body used for frozen sections.

Name *Emma Laberge* *at 16*

    Received *22ʳᵈ January* 1884 *from* *Bon Pasteur*

Sex *Female* Religion *Rome* *Cause of Death*

Buried in the *Roman Catholic*   Cemetery on

the   188

REMARKS:

Name _Philomene Fournier_   **12**

     Received _January 22nd 1884_ from _Longue Pointe Asylum_

Sex _Female_ Religion _Rome_ Cause of Death

Buried in the _Roman Catholic_   Cemetery on

the   188

REMARKS:

Buried as No 21

Name _Eliza Vane_

     Received _Feb 4th_   1884 from _Longue Pointe Asylum_

Sex _Female_ Religion _Protestant_ Cause of Death

Buried in the _Mount Royal_   Cemetery on

the   188

REMARKS:

Name _Joseph Goderre_

     Received _Feb 8th_ 1884 from _Hotel Dieu_

Sex _Male_ Religion _Rome_ Cause of Death

Buried in the _Roman Catholic_   Cemetery on

the   188

REMARKS:

Name *George Thomas* 13
Received *Feb 8th* 1884 *from* *Hotel Dieu*
Sex *Male* Religion *Rome* Cause of Death
Buried in the *Roman Catholic* Cemetery on
the _____ 188

REMARKS:

Name *William Fraser*
Received *February 26th* 1884 *from* *Montreal General Hospital*
Sex *Male* Religion *Protestant* Cause of Death
Buried in the *Mount Royal* Cemetery on
the _____ 188

REMARKS:

Name *Joseph Petit - dit la Lumiere*
Received *March 4th* 1884 *from* *Longue Pointe Asylum*
Sex *Male* Religion *Rome* Cause of Death
Buried in the *Roman Catholic* Cemetery on
the _____ 188

REMARKS:

Name *Henry Thomas*
  Received *March 6th 1884* *18th* *from* *Verdue Pointe Asylum*
Sex *Male* Religion *Protestant* *Cause of Death*
Buried in the *Mount Royal Cemetery* – Cemetery on
the _____ 188 _____

REMARKS:

Name *James Doherty*
  Received *March 10th* 1884 *from* *Montreal General Hospital*
Sex *Male* Religion *Protestant* *Cause of Death*
Buried in the *Mount Royal* _____ Cemetery on
the _____ 188 _____

REMARKS:

Name *Pierre Picard.*
  Received *March 10th* 1884 *from* *Hospice St Charles*
Sex *Male* Religion *Rome* *Cause of Death*
Buried in the *Roman Catholic* Cemetery on
the _____ 188 _____

REMARKS:

Name *Joseph Poirier*
Received *March 2 5th* 188 *4* from *Longue Pointe Asylum*
Sex *Male* Religion *Rome* Cause of Death
Buried in the *Roman Catholic* Cemetery on
the _____ 188

REMARKS:

Name *An unknown man – James Reid?*
Received 188 from *Montreal General Hospital*
Sex Religion Cause of Death
Buried in the *Roman Catholic* Cemetery on
the 188

REMARKS:

Name *André Roch*
Received *4 April* 188 *4* from *Hotel Dieu*
Sex *Male* Religion *Rome* Cause of Death
Buried in the *Roman Catholic* Cemetery on
the 188

REMARKS:

Name *Thomas Auger*
    Received *April 16th* 1884 from *Montreal General Hospital*
Sex *Male* Religion *Rome* Cause of Death
Buried in the *Roman Catholic* Cemetery on
the _____ 188

REMARKS:

Name *Margaret Gagné*
    Received *April 15th* 1884 from *Bon Pasteur*
Sex *Female* Religion *Rome* Cause of Death
Buried in the *Roman Catholic* Cemetery on
the _____ 188

REMARKS:

Name *Janet Rankley*
    Received *June 10* 1884 from *Longue Pointe Asylum*
Sex *Female* Religion *Ch England* Cause of Death *Epilepsy*
Buried in the ~~Roman Catholic~~ *Mount Royal* Cemetery on
the _____ 188

REMARKS:

Name *Mrs Maud Clark*

Received *June 12th* 1884 *from Montreal General Hospital*

Sex *Female* Religion *Rome* Cause of Death

Buried in the *Roman Catholic* Cemetery on

the *28th March* 1885

Name *George Hughes,*

Received *June 2nd* 1884 *from Longue Pointe Asylum,*

Sex *Male* Religion *Rome* Cause of Death —

Buried in the *Roman Catholic* Cemetery on

the *28th March* 1885

Name *Leocadie Piquette*
    Received *June 17th* 188**4** *from* *Mercy Pointe Asylum*
Sex *Female* *Religion* *Rome* *Cause of Death* —
Buried in the *Roman Catholic*   *Cemetery on*
the *28th March* . 188**5**
         REMARKS:

Name *Alexander Pearson*
    Received *June 23rd* 1884 *from* *Hotel Dieu*
Sex *Male* *Religion* *Rome* *Cause of Death*
Buried in the *Roman Catholic* —————*Cemetery on*
the *Immediately after its receipt owing to its being*
decomposed.   REMARKS:

Name *Frederic Geneveau*
    Received *July 2nd* 1884 *from* *Mercy Pointe Asylum*
Sex *Male* *Religion* *Rome* *Cause of Death*
Buried in the *Roman Catholic* ——— ——*Cemetery on*
the   188
         REMARKS:

Name *Lawrence Maher*

Received *Sept 22nd* 1884 from *Montreal Gaol*.

Sex *Male* Religion *Rome* Cause of Death *Phthisis*

Buried in the *Roman Catholic* Cemetery on

the _____ 188

REMARKS:

Name *Angelique Boucher*

Received *Sept 21st* 1884 from *Hospice St Charles*

Sex *Female* Religion *Rome* Cause of Death

Buried in the *Roman Catholic.* Cemetery on

the _____ 188

REMARKS:

the _____ 188

REMARKS:

Name —— Shepherd

    Received Sept 29th 1884 *from* Montreal General Hospital

Sex Male *Religion* Rome *Cause of Death* Heart Disease

Buried in the Roman Catholic _____ *Cemetery on*

the 188

REMARKS:

Name Eleas Mauriel

    Received Sept 29 1884 *from* Montreal Gaol.

Sex Male *Religion* Rome *Cause of Death*

Buried in the Mount Royal Cemetery. *Cemetery on*

the 188

REMARKS:

Name *Rose Ann Wallace* 21

    Received *Sept 30th* 1884 *from* *Hotel Dieu*

Sex **Female** *Religion* **Rome** *Cause of Death*

Buried in the **Roman Catholic**   *Cemetery on*

the   188

REMARKS:

Name **Nazaire Dube**

    Received *Oct 4th* 1884 *from* **Longue Pointe Asylum**

Sex **Male** *Religion* **Rome** *Cause of Death*

Buried in the **Roman Catholic** _____ *Cemetery on*

the   188

REMARKS:

Name **Gilbert Rochon**

    Received *October 9th* 1884 *from* **Hotel Dieu**

Sex **Male** *Religion* **Rome** *Cause of Death* —

Buried in the **Roman Catholic**   *Cemetery on*

the   188

REMARKS:

Name *Leandre Bertrand*

Received *Oct 15th* 1884 from *Hotel Dieu*

Sex *Male* Religion *Rome* Cause of Death

Buried in the *Roman Catholic* ———————— Cemetery on

the *March 28th* 1885

REMARKS:

Name *Jean Baptiste Brucher*

Received *Oct 15th* 1884 from *Hotel Dieu*

Sex *Male* Religion *Rome* Cause of Death

Buried in the *Roman Catholic* Cemetery on

the *28th March* 1885

REMARKS:

Name *Angele Brunette*
Received *Nov 7th* 1884 from *Longue Pointe Asylum*
Sex *Male* Religion *Rome* Cause of Death
Buried in the *Roman Catholic* Cemetery on
the *8th 28th March* 1885

REMARKS:

Name *Charlotte Jacques.*
Received *Nov 13th* 1884 from *Longue Point Asylum*
Sex *Female* Religion *Rome* Cause of Death
Buried in the *Roman Catholic* Cemetery on
the *28th March* 1885

REMARKS:

Name *Margaret McCormack*

    Received *Nov 29th* 1884 *from* Longue Pointe Asylum

Sex *Female* Religion *Rome* Cause of Death

Buried in the *Roman Catholic Cemetery* Cemetery on

the *28th March* 1885

REMARKS:

Name *Cecile Laroche*

    Received *Dec 18th* 1884 *from* Longue Pointe Asylum

Sex *Female* Religion *Rome* Cause of Death

Buried in the *Roman Catholic* — Cemetery on

the *28th March* 1885

REMARKS:

Name *Annie Perron*

    Received *Dec 18th* 1884 *from* Longue Pointe Asylum

Sex *Female* Religion *Rome* Cause of Death —

Buried in the *Roman Catholic* Cemetery on

the *28th March* 1885

REMARKS:

Name *Aglae Hebert*   25
   Received *Dec 23rd*   1884   *from* *Longue Pointe Asylum*
Sex *Female* Religion *Rome*   *Cause of Death*
Buried in the   *Roman Catholic* .   *Cemetery on*
the   *28th March*   188 5
                              REMARKS:

Name *Zoe Harnois*
   Received *Dec 24th* 1884 *from* *Gray nuns*
Sex *Female* Religion *Rome* *Cause of Death*
Buried in the   *Roman Catholic*   *Cemetery on*
the   *28th March* .   188 5
                              REMARKS:

Name *Theresa Gauthier dit - Landville*
   Received *Jan 10th*   1885 *from* *Asile de la Providence*
Sex *Female* Religion *Rome* *Cause of Death*   +
Buried in the   *Roman Catholic*   *Cemetery on*
the *March 28th*   188 5
                              REMARKS:

Name *Catherine Lucas*

    Received *Jan 13th*   1885 *from* *Argus Point Asylum*

Sex Female *Religion* Rome *Cause of Death*

Buried in the Roman Catholic   *Cemetery on*

the 28th March   1885

                 REMARKS:

Name Kate Crothy

    Received *Jan 14th*   1885 *from* Argus Point Asylum

Sex Female *Religion* Rome   *Cause of Death*

Buried in the Roman Catholic   *Cemetery on*

the 28 March   1885

                 REMARKS:

Name Angelina Huberdeault.

    Received *Jan 20th*   1885 *from* Argus Pointe Asylum

Sex Female *Religion* Rome *Cause of Death*

Buried in the Roman Catholic   *Cemetery on*

the 28th March.   1885

                 REMARKS:

Name *Louise Lapointe*

Received Jan 20th 1885 *from* Longue Pointe Asylum

Sex *Female* Religion *Rome* *Cause of Death*

Buried in the Roman Catholic *Cemetery on*

the 28th March 188

REMARKS:

Name *Joseph Labrecque*

Received Feb 2rd 1885 *from* Longue Point Asylum

Sex *Female* Religion *Rome* *Cause of Death* —

Buried in the Roman Catholic *Cemetery on*

the 28th March 188

REMARKS:

Name *Louise des Launiers*

Received Feb 2nd 1885 *from* Longue Pointe Asylum

Sex *Female* Religion *Rome* *Cause of Death*

Buried in the Roman Catholic *Cemetery on*

the 28th March 1885

REMARKS:

Name *Adeline Gendron*
    Received *February 25* 1885 *from Angne Pointe Asylum*
Sex *Female* Religion *Rome*   Cause of Death
Buried in the   *Roman Catholic*   Cemetery on
the   *28th March*   1885

REMARKS:

Name *Caroline Jerome*
    Received *March 5th* 1885 *from Angne Pointe Asylum*
Sex *Female* Religion *Rome*   Cause of Death
Buried in the   *Roman Catholic*   Cemetery on
the   *5th March*   1885

REMARKS:

Name *C. E. Bennett*
    Received *March 6th* 1885 *from Coroner*
Sex *Male* Religion ~~Rome~~ *Protestant* Cause of Death *Suicide - Pistol*
Buried in the   Cemetery on
the   188

REMARKS:

Received *March 11th* 188*5* from *Coroner*
Sex *Male* Religion *Protestant* Cause of Death *Suicide by hanging*
Buried in the _____ . Cemetery on
the _____ 188

REMARKS:

Name *Joseph Condon*
Received *March 30th* 188*5* from *Hôtel Dieu*
Sex *Male* Religion *Rome* Cause of Death
Buried in the *Roman Catholic* Cemetery on
the 188

REMARKS:

Name *Sophrenie Massé* æt 28.
Received *Apr 4th* 188*5* from *Hospice St Charles*
Sex *Female* Religion *Rome* Cause of Death
Buried in the *Roman Catholic* Cemetery on
the 188

REMARKS:

Name *Joseph Bousquet*
    Received *April 7th* 1885 from *Hôtel Dieu*
Sex *Male* Religion   Cause of Death
Buried in the   *Roman Catholic*   Cemetery on
the   188

REMARKS:

Name *Louis Quintal*
    Received *Apr 7th* 1885 from *Hôtel Dieu*
Sex *Male* Religion *Rome* Cause of Death
Buried in the *Roman Catholic*   Cemetery on
the   188

REMARKS:

Name *Thomas Browne*
    Received *April 14th* 1885 from *Montreal General Hospital*
Sex *Male* Religion *Ch. England* Cause of Death   —
Buried in the   ~~Roman Catholic~~ *Mount Royal* Cemetery on
the   188

REMARKS:

Name *Jane Leonard*   31

    Received *April 10th* 188 *5* *from* *Montreal General Hospital*

Sex *Female* Religion *Protestant* Cause of Death

Buried in the *Mount Royal* Cemetery on

the   188

REMARKS:

Name *Martin Carrick or Harrick*

    Received *April 22rd* 188 *5* *from* *Montreal Gaol*

Sex *Male* Religion *Rome* Cause of Death

Buried in the   Cemetery on

the   188

REMARKS:

Name *Joseph Latour*

    Received *May 4th.* 188 *5* *from* *Asile du Sacré Cœur*

Sex *Male* Religion *Rome* Cause of Death

~~Buried in the~~ *Was Taken away being unfit for* ~~Cemetery on~~

~~the~~ *dissection*   ~~188~~

~~REMARKS:~~

Name *John Farrell*
Received May 18th 1885 from *Hotel Dieu*
Sex ~~Female~~ Religion *Rome* Cause of Death
~~Buried in the~~ *Body immediately buried being unfit* ~~Cemetery on~~
~~the~~ _____ . 188_

REMARKS:

Name *Charles Leonard*
Received *May 19th* 188 *5* from
Sex   Religion   Cause of Death
Buried in the _____   Cemetery on
the   188

REMARKS:

Name *Jane Carr*
Received *May 25th* 1885 from *Hotel Dieu*
Sex *Femal* Religion *Rome* Cause of Death
Buried in the *Roman Catholic*   Cemetery on
the _____   188

REMARKS:

Name *Louis Daundurand*
Received *July 31st* 188 5 *from* *Gray Nuns*
Sex *Male* Religion *Rome* Cause of Death
Buried in the *Roman Catholic* Cemetery on
the 188

REMARKS:

Name *Rose Delima Allard*
Received *Aug 11th* 188 5 *from* *Bon Pasteur*
Sex *Female* Religion *Rome* Cause of Death
Buried in the *Roman Catholic* Cemetery on
the 188

REMARKS:

Name *William Murray*   **34**

     Received *August 11* 188*5* from *Montreal General Hospital*

Sex *Male* Religion *Protestant* Cause of Death

Buried in the *Roman Mount Royal* Cemetery on

the _____ 188

REMARKS:

Name *Andre Coquart*

     Received *August 18th* 188*5* from *Hotel Dieu*

Sex *Male* Religion *Rome* Cause of Death —

Buried in the *Roman Catholic* Cemetery on

the 188

REMARKS:

Name *Catherine Daley*

     Received *Aug 21st* 188*5* from *Hotel Dieu*

Sex *Female* Religion *Rome* Cause of Death

Buried in the *Roman Catholic* Cemetery on

the 188

REMARKS:

Name *Caroline Read*

Received *September 10th* 188**5** *from* *Hôtel Dieu*

Sex *Female* Religion *Rome* Cause of Death

Buried in the *Roman Catholic* Cemetery on

the _____ 188___

REMARKS:

Name *Joseph Senecal*

Received *Sept 16th* 188**5** *from* *Notre Dame Hospital*

Sex *Male* Religion *Rome* Cause of Death

Buried in the *Roman Catholic* Cemetery on

the _____ 188___

REMARKS:

Name *Frank Shee*

Received *Oct 25th* 1885 from *Montreal General Hospital*

Sex *Male* Religion *Rome* Cause of Death

Buried in the *Roman Catholic* Cemetery on

the _____ 188

REMARKS:

Name *Nicolas Hurtubise*

Received *Nov 6th* 1885 from *Gray Nuns*

Sex *Male* Religion *Rome* Cause of Death *Old age at 104*

Buried in the *Roman Catholic* Cemetery on

the _____ 188

REMARKS:

Name _William Perley_   37
 Received _November 17th_ 188**5** _from_ _Sherbrooke_
Sex _Male_ Religion _Unknown_ *Cause of Death*
Buried in the _Mount Royal_   *Cemetery on*
the _____ 188

REMARKS:

Name _George McCurdy._
 Received _Nov 17th_ 188**5** _from_ _Montreal General Hospital_
Sex _Male_ Religion _Rome_ *Cause of Death*
Buried in the _____ *Cemetery on*
the _____ 188

REMARKS:

Name _Patrick Quinn_
 Received _Nov 30th_ 188**5** _from_ _Longue Pointe Asylum_
Sex _Male_ Religion _Rome_ *Cause of Death*
Buried in the _Roman Catholic_   *Cemetery on*
the _____ 188

REMARKS:

Name George Pangborn
Received Dec 23rd 1885 *from* Anepe Pointe Asylum
Sex Male *Religion* Protestant *Cause of Death*
Buried in the Roman Catholic *Cemetery on*
the 188

REMARKS:

Name Philomene Riendeau
Received Dec 23rd 1885 *from* Anepe Pointe Asylum
Sex Female *Religion* Rome *Cause of Death* —
Buried in the Roman Catholic *Cemetery on*
the 188

REMARKS:

Name *Catherine Brazeau*

Received *Jan 17th* 188*6* from *Longue Pointe Asylum*

Sex *Female* Religion *Rome* Cause of Death

Buried in the *Roman Catholic* Cemetery on

the _____ 188

REMARKS:

Name *Joseph Blake*

Received *Jan 18th* 188*6* from *Longue Pointe Asylum*

Sex *Male* Religion *Protestant* Cause of Death

Buried in the *Mount Royal* Cemetery on

the _____ 188

REMARKS:

Name *Albion North.*

Received *Jan 20th* 188*6* from *Longue Pointe Asylum*

Sex *Male* Religion *Protestant Presbyterian* Cause of Death

Buried in the *Roman Cath Mount Royal* Cemetery on

the _____ 188

REMARKS:

Name *Joseph Contras*

Received *Feb 5th* 188 *6* from *Longue Pointe Asylum*

Sex *Male* Religion *Rome* Cause of Death

Buried in the *Roman Catholic* Cemetery on

the   188

REMARKS:

Name *Jeremie Rene*

Received *Feb 12th* 188 *6* from *Longue Pointe Asylum*

Sex *Male* Religion *Rome* Cause of Death

Buried in the *Roman Catholic* Cemetery on

the   188

REMARKS:

Name *Bridget O'Keefe*

Received *Feb 15th* 188*6* *from* *Montreal General Hospital*.

Sex *Female* Religion *Rome* Cause of Death

Buried in the *Roman Catholic* Cemetery on

the 188

REMARKS:

Name *Alexis Lafleur,*

Received *February 27th* 188*6* *from* *Montreal Gaol*

Sex *Male* Religion *Rome* Cause of Death

Buried in the *Roman Catholic Ce* Cemetery on

the *31st December* 188*5.*

REMARKS:

Name _Mary Reid_

86-87 / 22 / 2"

Received _March 3rd_ 1886 _from_ Longue Point Asylum

Sex _Female_ Religion _Protestant_ Cause of Death

Buried in the _Protestant Cemetery_ ~~Cemetery~~ on

the _7th April March 2 6_ 188_6_.

REMARKS:

Operation Sis. 1886 -

Name —— _Hazleton._

Received _March 8th_ 1886 _from_ Montreal General Hospital

Sex _Male_ Religion _Protestant_ Cause of Death. _Pneumonia._

Buried in the ~~Mo~~ _Mount Royal_ Cemetery on

the _7th April_ 1886

Operative Surgery -

REMARKS:

Name _Rose Desjardins_

Received _March 13th_ 1886 _from_ Longue Pointe Asylum

Sex _Female_ Religion _Rome_ Cause of Death

Buried in the _Roman Catholic_ Cemetery on

the ~~13th March~~ _7th April_ 188_6_

REMARKS:

No 12 -

Name _William Ricketts_
Received _March 15th_ 188_6_ from _Montreal General Hospital_
11. Sex _Male_ Religion _Rome_ Cause of Death _Strangulated Hernia_
Buried in the _Roman Catholic_ Cemetery on
the _31st December_ 188_6_.

REMARKS:

Coloured.
_No 11._

Name — _Bartlett_
Received _March 16th_ 188 6 from _Montreal General Hospital._
Sex _Male_ Religion _Protestant_ Cause of Death _Alcoholism_
Buried in the _____ Cemetery on
the _____ 188

REMARKS:

Dissected in Summer Session.

Name _Delphine Riopel_
Received _March 27th_ 188_6_ from _Longue Pointe Asylum_
Sex _Female_ Religion _Rome_ Cause of Death
Buried in the _Roman Catholic_ Cemetery on
the _26th March_ 188_7_

REMARKS:

Xmas 4.

✳ Here there should have been entered. Roberge.
Genereux
Forget
McPhee
Laplante
McClare
Swinbright
Kanisentha
Theodore Leblanc
Mornsey
Barnett.

44

Name *Adele Laingue*
CHAP 3.
Received *April 2nd / 1886* 188 *from* Longue Pointe Asylum
Sex *Female* Religion *Rome* Cause of Death
Buried in the *Roman Catholic* Cemetery on
the *26th March* 1887
✻ *Xmas III* REMARKS:

Name *Thomas Brunette — (Shoemaker)*
CHAP 2.
Received *June 2nd* 1886 *from* Montreal Gaol
Sex *Male* Religion *Rome* Cause of Death *Paralysis*
Buried in the *Roman Catholic* Cemetery on
the *26th March* 188 7
Xmas II REMARKS:

Name *Scholastic Malboeuf at 70-*
CHAP I.
Received *June 10th* 1886 *from* Longue Pointe Asylum
Sex *Male* Religion *Rome* Cause of Death
Buried in the *Roman Catholic* Cemetery on
the *26th March* 1887
Xmas I REMARKS:

Name _John Preston_ æt 59
Received _June 17th_ 188_6_ from _Longue Pointe Asylum_
Sex _Male_ Religion _Rome_ Cause of Death
Buried in the _Roman Catholic_ Cemetery on
the _31st December_ 188_6_

No 6.

REMARKS:

Name _Francis Gallagher_ æt 45
Received _June 19th_ 1886 from _Montreal Gaol_
Sex _Male_ Religion _Rome_ Cause of Death _General Debility_
Buried in the _Roman Catholic_ Cemetery on
the _3rd December_ 1886.

REMARKS:

Name _Mary Campbell_
Received _Sept 6th_ 188_6_ from _Longue Pointe Asylum_
Sex _Female_ Religion _Rome_ Cause of Death
Buried in the _Roman Catholic_ Cemetery on
the _3rd December_ 188_6._

REMARKS:

46

Name *Wm McDermott*
Received *Sept 24th* 1886 *from Montreal General Hospital*
Sex *Male* Religion *Rome* Cause of Death *Phthisis*
Buried in the *Roman Catholic* Cemetery on
the *21 December* 1886.

REMARKS:
No 2.; Died in my wards in M.G.H. Was a deaf mute. Buried as No 2.

Name *Pélagie Planté.*
Received *Sept 27th* 1886 *from Longue Pointe Asylum*
Sex *Female*. Religion *Rome* Cause of Death
Buried in the *Roman Catholic* Cemetery on
the *31st December* 1886.

REMARKS:
Buried as No 1. Oct 1886

Name *Jean Dufresne*
Received *Oct 7th* 1886 *from Longue Pointe*
Sex *Male* Religion *Rome* Cause of Death
Buried in the *Roman Catholic* Cemetery on
the *Dec 31st* 1886.

REMARKS:
No 7 Buried. buried Oct 8th

Received Oct 13th 1886 from Hôtel Dieu
Sex Male Religion Rome Cause of Death Pneumonia
Buried in the Roman Catholic Cemetery on
the 26th March 1887

REMARKS:
Dr Shepherds autopsy

Name J. J. Sullivan
Received Oct 25th 1886 from Montreal General Hospital
Sex Male Religion Protestant Cause of Death Phthisis
Buried in the Protestant Cemetery on
the 26th March 1887

No 23
REMARKS:

Name Sarah McEwan
Received Oct 25th 1886 from Montreal General Hospital
Sex Female Religion Rome Cause of Death Bronchitis
Buried in the Cemetery on
the Nov 18th 1886

REMARKS:
Autopsy Aft Reclaimed & thrown night Nov 7th
& given up to her son.

Name *Elmire Lebrus*   48

    Received *Nov 1st* 188**6** *from Longue Pointe Asylum*

No 9   Sex *Female* Religion *Rome* Cause of Death -

    Buried in the *Roman Catholic*   Cemetery on

    the   *31st December* 188 **6** -

Subject 10. , *Very thin. Body covered with petechiae* .   REMARKS:

Name *Mary Sutton*

    Received *Nov 12th* 1886 *from Montreal General Hospital*

15   Sex *Female* Religion *Rome* Cause of Death *Heart Disease* .

    Buried in the *Roman Catholic*   Cemetery on

    the *Dec 31st* 188 **6** ,

REMARKS:

Nov 15

Name *Pierre Roberge*

    Received *April 2rd* 188**6** *from Longue Pointe Asylum*

    Sex *Male* Religion *Rome* Cause of Death

    Buried in the   Cemetery on

    the   188

REMARKS:

Operative Surgery -

Name *Madame Genereux*
Received *April 10th* 188*6* from *Longue Pointe asylum*
Sex *Female* Religion *Rome* Cause of Death
Buried in the *Roman Catholic* Cemetery on
the *31 December* 188*6*

REMARKS:

A.

Name *Pierre Forget*
Received *April 27th* 188*6* from *Longue Pointe asylum*
Sex *Male* Religion *Rome* Cause of Death
Buried in the *Roman Catholic* Cemetery on
the *26th March* 188*7*

No 20 REMARKS:

Name *Margaret MacFee*
Received *April 27th* 188*6* from *Montreal General Hospital*
Sex *Male* Religion *Protestant* Cause of Death
Buried in the *Mount Royal* Cemetery on
the *26th March* 188*7*

No 16. REMARKS:

Name *Elzear Laplante*

Received *May 1st* 188 *6* from *Longue Pointe Asylum*

Sex *Male* Religion *Rome* Cause of Death

Buried in the *Roman Catholic* Cemetery on

the *31st December* 188 *6*

/4

REMARKS:

Name *Danul McClare.*

Received *May 14th* 188 *6* from *Hotel Dieu*

Sex *Male* Religion *Rome* Cause of Death

Buried in the *Roman Catholic* ————————Cemetery on

the *31st December* 188 *6*

/3

REMARKS:

Name *James Swinright*

Received *May 14th* 188 *6* from *Longue Pointe Asylum*

Sex *Male* Religion *Rome* Cause of Death

Buried in the *Roman Catholic* Cemetery on

the *26th March* 188 *7*

/9.

REMARKS:

Name _Anastasia Kaniseutha_
　　Received May 20th 188_ from _Longue Pointe Asylum_
Sex _Female_ Religion _Rome_ Cause of Death
Buried in the _____ Cemetery on
the _____ 31st December (?) 1886 .

REMARKS:
4 .

Name _Maxime Clement_
　　Received May 20th 1886 from _Lo.P. Asylum_
Sex _Male_ Religion _Rome_ Cause of Death
Buried in the _Roman Catholic_ Cemetery on
the _26th March_ 188_

REMARKS:
17

Name _Theodore Leblanc_
　　Received May 22nd 1886 from _Longue Pointe Asylum_
Sex _Male_ Religion _Rome_ Cause of Death
Buried in the _Roman Catholic_ Cemetery on
the _26th March_ 1887

REMARKS:
Xmas 5 .

Name _John Morrissey._ 52

Received May 22nd 188 6 from Longue Pointe Montreal General Hospital

Sex Male Religion Rome Cause of Death

Buried in the Roman Catholic Cemetery on

the 26th March 1887

REMARKS:

No 18

Name Mary Jane Barnett

Received May 24th 1886 from Longue Pointe Asylum

Sex Female Religion Protestant Cause of Death

Buried in the Mount Royal Cemetery on

the March 26th 1887

REMARKS:

Name Jean Baptiste Jacques

Received Sept 9th 188 6 from Notre Dame Hospital

Sex Female Religion Rome Cause of Death

Buried in the Roman Catholic Cemetery on

the 26th March 1887

REMARKS:

25

Name _Margaret Robinson_   53
    Received _November 17th_ 188_6_ from _Montreal Gen'l Hospital_
Sex _Female_ Religion _Protestant_ Cause of Death _Paraplegia_
Buried in the _Roman Catholic Mount Royal_ Cemetery on
the _26th March_ 188_7_

REMARKS:

a P.M. had been made.

Name _Cornelius Flint_
    Received _November 23rd_ 188_6_ from _Montreal General Hospital_
Sex _Male_ Religion _Rome_ Cause of Death _Pneumonia_
Buried in the _Roman Catholic_ Cemetery on
the _March 26th_ 188_7_

REMARKS:

Xmas 7

Name _May Leonard_
    Received _Nov 29th_ 188_6_ from _Montreal General Hospital_
Sex _Female_ Religion _Rome_ Cause of Death _Paralysis_
Buried in the _Roman Catholic_ Cemetery on
the _March 26th_ 188_7_

REMARKS:

_26_

Name *Angela Bonvendi* 54

Received Dec 4th 7 188 6 *from* Montreal General Hospital

Sex *Male* Religion *Rome* *Cause of Death* Phthisis

Buried in the *Roman Catholic* Cemetery on

the *March 26* 188 7

REMARKS:

Name *George Brusso or Busso*

Received Dec 13th 188 *from* Montreal General Hospital

Sex *Male* Religion *Rome* *Cause of Death* Phthisis

Buried in the *Roman Catholic* Cemetery on

the *26th March* 188 7

REMARKS:

Name *Jerome Blanchette*

Received Jan 22nd 188 7 *from* Montreal Gaol

Sex *Male* Religion *Catholic* *Cause of Death* Debility

Buried in the *Roman Catholic* Cemetery on

the *26th March* 188 7

REMARKS:

Name *Samuel Jackson*

taken away by relatives. Received *Feb 16th* 188*7* from *Montreal General Hospital*

Sex *Male* Religion *Baptist* Cause of Death *Pneumonia* –

Buried in the _____ Cemetery on

the _____ 188___

REMARKS:

Was given up to his relatives – I refunded to his widow the
$11 which had been paid. & the Lamorande remitted $5 on
the price of the next Subject.

Name *John Higgins*

Received *February 23d* 1887 from *Montreal General Hospital*

Sex *Male* Religion *Rome* Cause of Death *Phthisis*

Buried in the *Roman Catholic* Cemetery on

the *22 July* 188*7*.

To be used for *Steams*. REMARKS:

R C.

~~Alexis Lafleur~~
Delphine Prosperosse
Adèle Lacigne
Thomas Brunette ?
Scholastique Martin?
Patrick Smith
Pierre Forget
James Swinright
Maxime Clement
Theodore Leblanc
John Morrissey
J. B. Jacques
Cornelius Flint
Mary Leonard
Angela Bonvendi
George Russo
Jerome Blanchette

Prot.

Mary Reid
T. J. Sullivan
Margaret Mc Phee
Mary Jane Barnett
Margaret Robinson
Helena Leslie

March 2 6. 1887

Name *Paul Lajoie*
    Received *Feb 26th* 188**7** from *Longue Pointe Asylum*
Sex *Male* Religion *Rome* Cause of Death *Epilepsy.*
Buried in the   Cemetery on
the   188

REMARKS:

Used for Examination in Anatomy and subsequently for No 27 in 1887-88

Name *James Clury*
    Received *March 9th* 188**7** from *Montreal General Hosp.*
Sex *Male* Religion *Rome* Cause of Death
Buried in the *Roman Catholic* Cemetery on
the *22nd July* 188**7**

REMARKS:

No 26

Name *Simon Paquet*
    Received *March 21st* 188 from *Hotel Dieu*
Sex *Male* Religion *Rome* Cause of Death *Bronchitis*
Buried in the *Roman Catholic* Cemetery on
the *22nd July* 188**7**.

REMARKS:

Extra 1 —

Rome.

John Higgins
Paul Lajoie
James Clery
Simon Paquet

Received 22ᵈ /8
July

Name *Marguerite Poirier*

    Received *25th March* 1887 *from* *Hospice St Charles*

Sex *Female* Religion *Rome* Cause of Death

Buried in the *Roman Catholic*   Cemetery on

the *22nd December* 1887

No. 10.   REMARKS:

Name *Henry Jackson Goddard*

    Received *March 25th* 1887 *from* *Montreal Genl Hospital.*

Sex *Male* Religion *Ch: England* Cause of Death *Rupture of Urethra*

Buried in the *Mount Royal Cemetery*   Cemetery on

the *22nd December* 1887.

     REMARKS:

Surgery

Name *Merance Brouillet* (?)

    Received *April 2nd* 1887 *from* *Longue Pointe Asylum*

Sex *Male* Religion *Rome* Cause of Death *"Marasme"*

Buried in the *Roman Catholic*   Cemetery on

the *22nd December* 1887

     REMARKS:

No 11.

Name *Robert Irving* 58

 Received *April 5th* 1887 from *Montreal General Hospital*

Sex *Male* Religion *Presbyterian* Cause of Death *Debility and Erysipelas.*

Buried in the   Cemetery on

the   188

REMARKS:

No 21.

Name *James Parr*

 Received *April 5th* 1887 from *Montreal General Hospital*

Sex *Male* Religion *Ch England* Cause of Death *Phthisis*

Buried in the   Cemetery on

the   188

REMARKS:

No 22.

Name *Kate Loyce*

 Received *April 5th* 1887 from *Hotel Dieu*

Sex *Female* Religion *Rome* Cause of Death *Phthisis*

Buried in the   Cemetery on

the   188

REMARKS:

No 24.

Name _William King_ 59

Received _April 18th - 1887_ from _Montreal General Hospital_

Sex _Male_ Religion _Ch England_ Cause of Death _Fracture of Skull_

Buried in the _Mount Royal_ Cemetery on

the _22nd December_ 1888.

REMARKS:

_No 14._

Name _George Tyrell_

Received _April 20th_ 1887 from _Montreal General Hospital_

Sex _Male_ Religion _Ch England_ Cause of Death _Nephritis_

Buried in the _Mount Royal_ Cemetery on

the _22nd December_ 1886

REMARKS:

Extra iii

Name _Joseph Gregroire_

Received _April 30th_ 1887 from _Hospice St Charles_

Sex _Male_ Religion _Rome_ Cause of Death _Pneumonia_

Buried in the _Roman Catholic_ Cemetery on

the _22nd_ 188

REMARKS:

_No 7._

Name _Dufault - Veuve Pierre Turcotte_   60

Received _Apr 30th_ 188**7** from _Grey Nunnery_ -

Sex _Female_ Religion _Rome_ Cause of Death _old age_ -

Buried in the _Roman Catholic_   Cemetery on

the _22nd December_ . 188**7**.

No _12_,   REMARKS:

Name _Marie Gagnier_

Received _April 27th_ 188**7** from _Longue Pointe Asylum_

Sex _Female_ Religion _Rome_ Cause of Death _Erysipelas_ -

Buried in the _Roman Catholic_   Cemetery on

the _22nd December_ 188**7**

No _19_,   REMARKS:

Name _Enelda Tourville_

Received _6 May_ 188**7** from _Hotel Dieu_

Sex _Female_ Religion _Rome_ Cause of Death _Pneumonia_

Buried in the _Roman Catholic_   Cemetery on

the _16th March_ 188**8**

No _20_.   REMARKS:

Dec 22nd 1887.

Gave orders for the Burial of

Protestant 1. George Tyrrell
                 2. William King
                 3. Henry Goddard

R C

1. George Pitaway
2. François Brunelle
3. Hermina Gaucher
4. Catherine McGuire
5. Marie Carrière
6. Mary Shehyn
7. Joseph Gregoire
8. Geneviève du Bois
9. Charles Lavine
10. Joseph Beaudamon
11. Marguerite Poirier
12. Merence Brouillet
13. Dame Turcotte
14. Marie Gagner
15. Ann Bourke
16. Ann O'Connor
17. Antoine Raymond

Name *Catherine Lynch*

Received 4th ~~May~~ May 13th 1887 from *Hôtel Dieu* —

Sex *Female* Religion *Rome* *Cause of Death* *Pericarditis*

Buried in the *Roman Catholic* Cemetery on

the *March 16th* 1888

No. 19.

REMARKS:

Name *Joseph Duclos*

Received *May 21st* 1887 from *Hôtel Dieu*

Sex *Male* Religion *Rome* Cause of Death *Paralysis*

Buried in the *Roman Catholic Cemetery* Cemetery on

the *March 16th* 1888.

No 18

REMARKS:

Name *Mary Rowe*

Received *June 10th* 1887 from *Montreal General Hospital*

Sex *Female* Religion *Ch England* Cause of Death *Phthisis*

Buried in the *Mount Royal* Cemetery on

the *16th March* 1888

No 17.

REMARKS:

Name *Rosanna Bombardier*
Received *June 13th* 1887 from *Longue Pointe asylum*
Sex *Female* Religion *Rome* Cause of Death *Marasmus*
Buried in the *Roman Catholic* Cemetery on
the *16th March* 188

REMARKS:

Christmas 2.

Name *Marguerite Latulife*
Received *June 15th* 1887 from *Mr Gray Nuns.*
Sex *Female* Religion *Rome* Cause of Death *Paralysis*
Buried in the *Roman Catholic* Cemetery on
the *16th March* 1888

REMARKS:

Christmas 4

Name *Mary Shehyn*
Received *Sept 10th* 1887 from *Montreal General Hospital*
Sex *Female* Religion *Rome* Cause of Death *Phthisis*
Buried in the *Roman Catholic* Cemetery on
the *22nd December* 1888.

REMARKS:

No 6.

Name _Marie Carrière_ **63**

  Received _16th Sept r_ 1887 _from Longue Pointe Asylum._

Sex _Female_ Religion _Rome_ Cause of Death _"Marasme"_

Buried in the _Roman Catholic_   Cemetery on

the _22nd December_   1887.

_No 5._

      REMARKS:

Name _George Pitaway_

  Received _20th September_ 1887 _from Hôtel Dieu._

Sex _male_ Religion _Rome_ Cause of Death

Buried in the _Roman Catholic_   Cemetery on

the _22nd December_   1887

_No 1._

      REMARKS:

Name _Hermina Gaucher_

  Received _20th Sept_ 1887 _from Longue Pointe Asylum_

Sex _Female_ Religion _Rome_ Cause of Death

Buried in the _Roman Catholic_   Cemetery on

the _22nd December_   1887

_No 3._

      REMARKS:

Name _Francois Brunette_
Received 26th September 1887 from _Longue Pointe Asylum_
Sex _Male_ Religion _Rome_ Cause of Death
Buried in the _Roman Catholic_ Cemetery on
the _22rd December_ 1887

REMARKS:

No 2

Name _Julia Lefevre_
Received 3rd Oct 1887 from _Hotel Dieu_
Sex _Female_ Religion _Rome_ Cause of Death _Cancer of Uterus_
Buried in the _Roman Catholic_ Cemetery on
the _16th March_ 1888

REMARKS:

Christian 3.

Name *Genevieve duBois*

Received *10 Oct* 1887 *from* *Hospice St Charles*

Sex *Female* Religion *Rome* Cause of Death

Buried in the *Roman Catholic Cemetery* Cemetery on

the ~~10th March~~ *22rd Dec* 1888

No 8

REMARKS:

Name *Charles Lavine*

Received *17th Oct* 1887 *from* *Montreal General Hospital*

Sex *Male* Religion *Rome* Cause of Death *Fract Skull.*

Buried in the *Roman Catholic* Cemetery on

the *22nd Dec* 1888

No Extra 2

REMARKS:

Name *Ann Burke*

Received *Oct 21st* 1887 *from* *Montreal General Hosp*

Sex *Female* Religion *Rome* Cause of Death *Heart Disease*

Buried in the *Roman Catholic* Cemetery on

the *22rd December* 1887.

No 15.

REMARKS:

Name *Ann O'Connor*

    Received *Oct 29th* 188 7 *from Longue Pointe Asylum*

Sex *Female* Religion *Rome* Cause of Death *Cerebral Laemorhage*

Buried in the *Roman Catholic* Cemetery on

the ~~21st~~ *22nd November* 188 9

    REMARKS:

No 16

Name *Joseph Brindamon*

    Received *nov 5th* 1887 *from Longue Pointe Asylum*

Sex *Male* Religion *Rome* Cause of Death *General debility*

Buried in the *Roman Catholic* Cemetery on

the *22nd ~~March~~ December* 188 9

    REMARKS:

No 9

Name *Thomas Doran*

    Received *9th November* 1887 *from Longue Pointe Asylum*

Sex *Male* Religion *Rome* Cause of Death *General Debility*

Buried in the *Roman Catholic* Cemetery on

the *22nd December* 188 9

    REMARKS:

No known

Dr Shepherds subject

Name *Jennie Wilson*

Received Nov 1st 1887 from Montreal General Hospital

Sex *Female* Religion *Rome* Cause of Death *Cancer*

Buried in the *Roman Catholic* Cemetery on

the ~~22nd December 1887~~ 16th March 1888

~~No. 4.~~ Remark 4.

Name *Tharcile Parent Srinise de J Versailles*

Received Dec 12th 1887 from *Hospice de la miséricorde*

Sex *Female* Religion *Rome* Cause of Death *Puerperal Fever.*

Buried in the *Roman Catholic* Cemetery on

the 16th March 1888

No 23.

Name Jane Hetherington — **68**
Received Dec 15th 1887 from Montreal General Hospital
Sex Female **Religion** Rome **Cause of Death** Heart Disease.
Buried in the Roman Catholic **Cemetery on**
the 16th March 1888

REMARKS:
Christmas No 7.

Name Olaf Jansen
Received Dec 18th 1887 from Montreal General Hospital
Sex **Religion** Protestant **Cause of Death** Pneumonia.
Buried in the Mount Royal **Cemetery on**
the 16th March 1888

REMARKS:
Christmas Holiday No 6.

Name Henry Homan
Received Dec 27th 1887 from Montreal General Hospital
Sex Male **Religion** England **Cause of Death** Heart Disease.
Buried in the Mount Royal **Cemetery on**
the 6th January 1886.

REMARKS:
This body was given to the Rev. Mr. French for burial.
Mr F Paying all Expenses.

March 16th 1888

Gave order for the burial of

R. Catholic.

Kate Joyce
Joseph Gregoire
Etilda Jonville
Catherine Lynch
Joseph Duclos
Rosanna Bombardier
Marguerite Latulipe
Julia Lefevre
Jennie Wilson
Marvile Versailles
Jane Hetherington
Louis Gariepy
John Slater.

Protestants
Robert Irving
James Parr
Mary Rome
Olaf Jansen

R Macdonell

Name **Louis Gariepy**
Received Jan 3rd & 1887 from Montreal General Hospital
Sex Male Religion Rome Cause of Death Phthisis
Buried in the Roman Catholic Cemetery on
the 16th March 1887.

REMARKS:
Dr Shepherd's second subject.

Name **John Slater**
Received Jan 16th — 1888 from Montreal Gen Hospital
Sex Male Religion Rome Cause of Death Injury of Spine —
Buried in the Roman Catholic Cemetery on
the 16th March 1888

REMARKS:
Used partly for sections and the rest for No 25.

Name **John Norton or Naughton.**
Received Feb 4th — 1888 from Montreal General Hospital
Sex Male Religion Rome Cause of Death Cancer of liver
Buried in the Roman Catholic Cemetery on
the 16th March 1888

REMARKS:

No 28

Name   *Harriet Mannering.*

    Received   Feb 8th   188 8   *from* Longue Pointe Asylum

Sex *Female* Religion *Protestant* *Cause of Death*

Buried in the _____ Cemetery on

the _____ 188 _____

REMARKS:

Died by ... ...

Subjects for session of 1888 - 1889 from page 70
to " 84

Name   *John Logan.*

    Received   14th February 188 8   *from* Longue Pointe Asylum.

XVI Sex *Male* Religion *Rome* *Cause of Death* *Marasme.*

Buried in the _____ Cemetery on

the _____ 188 _____

REMARKS:

Name   *Margaret Burdles*

XVI **Received**   March 12th 188 8   *from* Gaol

Sex *Female* Religion *Rome* *Cause of Death* _____

Buried in the _____ Cemetery on

the _____ 188 _____

REMARKS:

Name *Philippe Begin*
Received *March 12ᵗʰ* 1888 from *Longue Pointe Asylum*
Sex *Female* Religion *Rome* Cause of Death *Typhoid fever*
Buried in the Cemetery on
the 188

REMARKS:

Name *Damase Fossard*
Received *March 14ᵗʰ* 1888 from *Grey Nuns*
Sex *Male* Religion *Rome* Cause of Death *Paralysis*
Buried in the *Roman Catholic* Cemetery on
the 188

REMARKS:

Used for Operative Surgery April 1888

Name *Catherine Pauliet*
Received *March 19ᵗʰ* 1888 from *Longue Pointe Asylum*
Sex *Female* Religion *Rome* Cause of Death *Tuberculosis*
Buried in the *Roman Catholic* Cemetery on
the 188

REMARKS:

Name *Alice Holman*

Received *March 19th* 188 from *Longue Pointe Asylum*

Sex *Female* Religion *Rome* Cause of Death *Marasmus*

Buried in the *Roman Catholic* Cemetery on

the _____ 188_____

REMARKS:

So rotten had to replace ē. Paul. Maillet

Name *Sarah Metry*

Received *April 9th* 188 from *Longue Pointe Asylum*

Sex *Female* Religion *Rome* Cause of Death *Debility.*

Buried in the *Roman Catholic* Cemetery on

the _____ 188_____

REMARKS:

Name *Mary Ann Smith*

Received *10th April* 188 from *Female Gaol*

Sex *24* Religion *Rome* Cause of Death *Consumption*

Buried in the *Roman Catholic* Cemetery on

the _____ 188_____

REMARKS:

Name _Laurent Crevier_

Received _April 12th_ 188**8** from _Hôtel Dieu_

Sex _Male_ Religion _Rome_ Cause of Death _Epithelioma.flip._

Buried in the _Roman Catholic Cemetery_ Cemetery on

the _____ 188

REMARKS:

Dr Shepherd's second subject for Operative Surgery.

Name _M. Brière_

Shared c̄ ʋShepherd and₋as Subject A. Received _April 19th_ 188**8** from _Hôpital Notre Dame_

Sex _Male_ Religion _Catholic_ Cause of Death _Ramollissement Cerebral_

Buried in the _Roman Catholic._ Cemetery on

the _____ 188

REMARKS:

Name _Joseph Brault_

Received _April 28th._ 188**8** from _Longue Pointe Asylum_

Sex _Female_ Religion _Rome_ Cause of Death _Senile Debility_

Buried in the _Roman Catholic_ Cemetery on

the _____ 188

REMARKS:

Name Marie Prevost.

Received May 1st 8... 1888 *from* Hôtel Dieu

Sex Female *Religion* Rome *Cause of Death* Phthisis

Buried in the Roman Catholic *Cemetery on*

the _____ 188____

REMARKS:

Name Daniel Cahill

Received May 8th 1888 *from* Longue Pointe Asylum

Sex Male *Religion* Rome *Cause of Death* Congestion cérébrale

Buried in the Roman Catholic. *Cemetery on*

the . _____ 188____

REMARKS:

Name _Onesime Hottin_

Received _May 12th_ 1888 _from_ _Longue Pointe Asylum_

Sex _Male_ Religion _Rome_ Cause of Death _Maladie du Cœur_

Buried in the _Roman Catholic_ ——————————Cemetery on

the _____ 188_

REMARKS:

Name _Judith Confield._

Received _May 12th_ 1888 _from_ _Longue Pointe Asylum_

Sex _Female_ Religion _Rome_ Cause of Death _Marasme Nerveuse._

Buried in the _Roman Catholic_ ——————————Cemetery on

the _____ 188_

REMARKS:

Name _Joseph Pacifie Harnois_

Received _May 15th_ 1888 _from_ _Longue Pointe Asylum_

Sex _Male_ Religion _Rome_ Cause of Death _General Paralysis_

Buried in the _Roman Catholic_ Cemetery on

the _____ 188_

REMARKS:

Pd fr by me

Name *Matilde Duquette*

Received *June 8th* 188 8 from *Notre Dame Hospital*

Sex *female* Religion *Rome* Cause of Death *Ht Disease*

Buried in the *Roman Catholic Cemetery* Cemetery on

the _____ 188

REMARKS:

Deth

Pd fr by me

Name *Marie La Liberté*

Received *June 15* 188 8 from *Longue Pointe Asylum*

Sex *Female* Religion *Catholic* Cause of Death —

Buried in the *Roman Catholic* Cemetery on

the _____ 188

REMARKS:

Paid £ J.J.S.

Name *Patrick Michael Kane*

Received *Sept 14th* 188 8 *from Longue Pointe Asylum*

Sex *Male* Religion *R. C.* Cause of Death *Debility*

Buried in the _____ Cemetery on

the _____ 188

№ I

REMARKS:

Name: *Joseph Riches*

Received *14/ 88* 188 *from Hotel Dieu*

Sex *Male* Religion *R. C.* Cause of Death *Bronchitis*

Buried in the _____ Cemetery on

the _____ 188

№ II

REMARKS:

Name *Sarah Smith.*
　　Received 188　 *from*
Sex *Female* Religion *R C*　 *Cause of Death*
Buried in the
the　　　　　　　　　　188
GivenREMARKS:
Given back to her sister.

Name *Statius Seratoos*
　　Received *25 Oct*　 188**8** *from* *Dr G. H.*
Sex *Male* Religion *Lutheran* *Cause of Death*
Buried in the　　　　　　　　*Cemetery on*
the　　　　　　　　188
REMARKS:

Name *Martin Geil*
　　Received *Oct 31.*　 188**8** *from* *Longue Pointe*
Sex *Male* Religion *R.C.* *Cause of Death* *Marasmus.*
Buried in the　　　　　　　　*Cemetery on*
the　　　　　　　　188
REMARKS:

Name *Rosalie Daragow* 68.

Received *10 Nov* 188 8 *from Convent of the Providence*

Sex *Female* Religion *Rome* Cause of Death *Inflam: y lungs.*

Buried in the   Cemetery on

the   188

REMARKS:

Name *Joseph Caillebout.* 16.

D. Shepherd **Received** *27 Nov* 188 8 *from Reformatory*

Sex *Male* Religion *R C.* Cause of Death *Phthisis*

Buried in the   Cemetery on

the   188

REMARKS:

Name *Henriette Hempey*

Received Dec 1 188 8 from Pnyne Pointe

Sex *Female* Religion *R.C.* Cause of Death *Paralysis*

Buried in the _____ Cemetery on

the _____ 188 ___

REMARKS:

Name *Paul Maillet*

Received 5 Dec 188 8 from Grey Nunnery

Sex *Male* Religion *RC* Cause of Death old age

Buried in the _____ Cemetery on

the _____ 188 ___

REMARKS:

XVI

Name *Thomas Baribault*
Received *3 Jany* 188*9* from *Hotel Dieu*
Sex *Male* Religion *R.C.* Cause of Death *Aneurysm*
Buried in the .... Cemetery on
the   188

REMARKS:

Name *Marie Bebn*
Received *7 Jany* 188 from *Hotel Dieu*
Sex *Female* Religion *R.C.* Cause of Death *Phthisis*
Buried in the .... Cemetery on
the   188

REMARKS:

Name *Cornelius Mcmaghan*

XX I

Received *22 Jany* 188 *9* from *M. G. Hospital*

Sex *Male* Religion *R.C.* Cause of Death *Pneumonia*

Buried in the _____ Cemetery on

the _____ 188

REMARKS:

Name *Vitaline Dupont* *61*

XX II

Received *6 Feb* 188 *9* from *Good Shepherd*

Sex *Female* Religion *R.C.* Cause of Death

Buried in the _____ Cemetery on

the _____ 188

REMARKS:

Name *Clara Cummings* 25

XXIV Received 6 Feb 188 9 from *M. G. H.*

Sex Female Religion Protestant Cause of Death *Phthisis*

Buried in the _____ Cemetery on

the _____ 188

REMARKS:

Name *Mary Bedford* 79.

R. Stephen physician Received 6 Feb 188 9 from *M. G. H.*

Sex Female Religion Protestant Cause of Death

Buried in the _____ Cemetery on

the _____ 188

REMARKS:

Name *Wm Taylor*   **84**

     Received *18 Feb*   1889   from *Longue Pointe Asylum*

Sex *Male* Religion *Protestant* Cause of Death

Buried in the   Cemetery on

the   188

REMARKS:

Subjects for session of 1889-1890. from page 84 to page —

Name *Joseph Brosseau*

     Received *8 Mch*   1889   from *Longue Pointe Asyl*

Sex *Male* Religion *R.C.*   Cause of Death *Typhoid*

Buried in the   Cemetery on

the   *30 July*   1889

REMARKS: *Spoilt*

Name *Ildérie le François*

     Received *Mch 8*   1889   from *Hotel Dieu*

Sex *Male* Religion *R.C.*   Cause of Death *Mitral Insufficiency*

Buried in the   Cemetery on

the   188

REMARKS:

Name Mary Lee

Received 14ᵗʰ Mch 1889 *from* Hotel Dieu

Sex Female *Religion* R.C. *Cause of Death* Phthisis

Buried in the   *Cemetery on*

the   30 July 188 9

REMARKS: Gratis

Name John Burns

Received 19ᵗʰ Mch 1889 *from* Hotel Dieu

Sex Male *Religion* R.C. *Cause of Death* Apoplexy

Buried in the   *Cemetery on*

the   30 July 188 9

REMARKS:

Name Christopher Russell.

No 1   **Received** 1 *April* 188**9** *from* M. G. H.

Operative Surgery *Sex* Male *Religion* RC. *Cause of Death*

Buried in the .... *Cemetery on*

the _____ 188

REMARKS:

Name Jos. Hay

X   **Received** 2 *April* 188**9** *from* M. G. H.

Sex Male *Religion* Interk *Cause of Death*

Buried in the .... *Cemetery on*

the 188

REMARKS:

Name *Rose Lebae*

Received *7 april* 188*9* *from* *Hospice St. Charles*

Se*x Female* Religion *R.C.* *Cause of Death*

Buried in the_____ *Cemetery on*

the _____ 188

REMARKS:

Name *Margaret St Cyr.*

Received *10 april* 188*9* *from* *Longue Pointe*

Sex *Female* Religion *R C* *Cause of Death*

Buried in the_____ *Cemetery on*

the_____ 188

REMARKS:

Name *James Dean* at 78.

Received *16 April* 188*9* from *Hotel Dieu*

Sex *Male* Religion *R.C.* Cause of Death *Bronchitis*

Buried in the_____ _____ Cemetery on

the _____ 188

Name *Delina Cloutier* 31

Received *16 April* 188*9* from *Hotel Dieu*

Sex *Female* Religion *R.C.* Cause of Death *Phthisis*

Buried in the_____ Cemetery on

the_____ 188

Returned to C. E. de Lamirande -

Name *Delina Roy*

     Received 26 April 188 9 from *Longue Pointe Asylum*

Sex *Female* Religion *R.C.* Cause of Death *Paralysis*.

Buried in the _____ Cemetery on

the _____ 188

REMARKS:

Name *J. B. Pirie*

     Received 27 April 188 9 from *Notre Dame Hospital*

Sex *Male* Religion *R.C.* Cause of Death *Pneumonia*.

Buried in the _____ Cemetery on

the _____ 188

REMARKS:

Name *Maria Irwin.*

Received *May 1st* 1889 from *Robt Dien*

Sex *Female* Religion *R.C.* Cause of Death *Phthisis*

Buried in the _____ Cemetery on

the _____ *30 July* 188 9

REMARKS: *Sprott*

Name *Marie Louise Le Marche*

Received *6 May* 1889 from *Hospice St Charles*

Sex *Female* Religion *R C.* Cause of Death *Debility*

Buried in the _____ Cemetery on

the _____ *30 July,* 188 9

REMARKS: *Sprott*

Name *Maurice O-Binn*

    Received *6 May*   188 9 *from* *Jail*

Sex .... *Religion* R C.   *Cause of Death* *Sudden*

Buried in the .... *Cemetery on*

the .... *3 July*   188 9

         REMARKS: . *Spoilt*

Name *Selina Guy*

    Received *14 May*   188 9 *from* *Hotel Dieu*

Sex *Female* *Religion* R C. *Cause of Death* *Pneumonia*

Buried in the .... *Cemetery on*

the .... *30 July*   188 9

         REMARKS: *Spoilt*

Name *Eugenie Dube*

    Received *May 14*   188 9 *from* *Hotel Dieu*

Sex .... *Religion* R C. *Cause of Death* *Phthisis*

Buried in the .... *Cemetery on*

the 188

         REMARKS:

Name *Charles Chouinard.*
Received *16 May* 188 9 from *Hôtel Dieu*
Sex *Male* Religion *R.C.* Cause of Death *Pneumonia.*
Buried in the   Cemetery on
the _____   188 _____

REMARKS:

Name *Ada Smith*
Received *19 May* 188 9 from *Longue Pointe*
Sex *Female* Religion *R.C.* Cause of Death *Cancer*
Buried in the   Cemetery on
the _____   188 _____

REMARKS:

Name *Emily McIntosh. 70.*
Received *27 May* 188 9 from *Longue Pointe*
Sex *Female* Religion *R.C.* Cause of Death *Debility*
Buried in the   Cemetery on
the _____   188 _____

REMARKS: *Subject previously marked XV. Abdomen s.*
and lower extremities were so rotten had to be
proportionately replaced by this.

Name *Joseph Lachance* 28.

Received 7 June 188 9 from *Longue Pointe*

Sex *Male* Religion *R.C.* Cause of Death *Debility*

Buried in the. Cemetery on

the 188

REMARKS:

Name *Mary Mc Govern*

Received 31 July 1889 from *Longue Pointe*

Sex *Female* Religion *R C.* Cause of Death *Phthisis*

Buried in the *R C* Cemetery on

the 26 mch 1890.

REMARKS:

Name *Celestin Holbrook*

Received *10 Aug.* 1889 from *Bayou Goula*

Sex *Female* Religion *R.C.* Cause of Death *Asthma*

Buried in the _____ Cemetery on

the _____ 188

REMARKS:

Name *Georgiana La Verrier*

Received *14 Aug* 1889 from *Bayou Goula*

Sex *Female* Religion *R.C.* Cause of Death *Phthisis*

Buried in the _____ Cemetery on

the _____ 188

REMARKS:

Name *Alphonse Gagnon*

Received 20 Aug 188 9 from *Hotel Dieu*

Sex *male* Religion *R C.* Cause of Death *Phthisis*

Buried in the _____ Cemetery on

the _____ 188

REMARKS:

Name *Anna Boucher*

Received 7 Sep' 188 9 from *M. G. Hospital*

Sex *Female* Religion *R C.* Cause of Death *Heart Disease*

Buried in the _____ Cemetery on

the _____ 188

REMARKS:

Name *Philomene Villemaire*

Received 28 Sept 1889 from *Longue Pointe*

Sex *Female* Religion *R.C.* Cause of Death *Marasme*

Buried in the _____ Cemetery on

the _____ 188

REMARKS:

Name *Emily Rousseau. 75.*

Received 28 Sept 1889 from *Longue Pointe*

Sex *Female* Religion *R.C.* Cause of Death *Cerebral Congestion*

Buried in the _____ Cemetery on

the _____ 188

REMARKS:

Name _Lizzie Smith_

Received _5 Oct_   188 _9_   from _Notre Dame Hospital_

Sex _Female_ Religion _R.C._   Cause of Death

Buried in the _____ _____ Cemetery on

the _____   188

REMARKS:

Name _Wm Buckley_

Received _Oct 24_ 188 _9_ from _M. G. H._

Sex _Male_ Religion _Protestant_ Cause of Death _Brights Disease_

Buried in the _Protestant_   Cemetery on

the _25 Oct_ 188 _9_

REMARKS:

(_Returned to friends_)

Name *Joseph François Allard*

Received 30 Nov 1889 from *Longue Pointe*

Sex *Male* Religion *R.C.* Cause of Death *Exhaustion*

Buried in the _____ Cemetery on

the _____ 188

REMARKS:

Name *Unknown*

Received 9 Dec 1889 from *Longue Pointe*

Sex *Male* Religion *R.C.* Cause of Death

Buried in the _____ Cemetery on

the _____ 188

REMARKS:

Name *Jean Parent*

Received 17 Dec. 1889 from *Longue Pointe*

Sex *Male* Religion *R C* Cause of Death

Buried in the _____ Cemetery on

the _____ 188__

REMARKS:

Name *Mary Ann McCullough*

Received 13 Dec 1889 from *Longue Pointe*

Sex *Female* Religion *R C* Cause of Death

Buried in the _____ Cemetery on

the _____ 188__

REMARKS:

Name *Adele Allen Cantin* at 33

Received 30 Dec 1889 from *Longue Point*

Sex *Female* Religion *R-C* Cause of Death

Buried in the ___ L C _____ Cemetery on

the ___ 26 Mch 1890

REMARKS:

Name *Mr. Goff*

Received *31 Dec* 188*9* from *M. G. H*

Sex *Female* Religion *Prot ?* Cause of Death

Buried in the _____ Cemetery on

the _____ 188

REMARKS:

Name *Mary O'Malley*

Received *9/1* 189*0* from *M. G. H.*

Sex *Female* Religion *R C* Cause of Death

Buried in the _____ Cemetery on

the _____ 188

REMARKS:

Name *Joel Rousselle* at 32.

Received *Feb. 10* 1890 from *Longue Pointe*

Sex *Male* Religion *R C* Cause of Death

Buried in the _____ _____ Cemetery on

the   188

REMARKS:

Name *Pepin née A. Lemire*

Received *Jany 28* 1890 from *Longue Pointe*

Sex _____ Religion *R C* Cause of Death _____

Buried in the _____   Cemetery on

the _____   188

REMARKS:

Name *John Morton*

Received *Jany 28* 18~~8~~90 . from *M. G. H*

Sex   Religion *P.*   Cause of Death

Buried in the _____ Cemetery on

the   188

REMARKS:

Name *Joseph Beauchamp.*

Received *Jany* 18~~8~~90 . from *Longue Pointe*

Sex _____ Religion *R C* ____ Cause of Death

Buried in the _____ Cemetery on

the _____ 188

REMARKS:

Name *Pierre Leroux.* æt 83,

Received *Feb* 1890. from *Jail*

Sex *Male* Religion *R C* Cause of Death

Buried in the _____ *R.* Cemetery on
the _____ *. . . . . . . Aug 28 / 9.* 188

REMARKS:

Name *James Goodrain. (Italian)*

Received *Mch 25* 1890 from *M. G. 76.*

Sex *Male* Religion *R C* Cause of Death _____

Buried in the *R C Cemeh* Cemetery on
the *Aug 26ᵗʰ* 1890

REMARKS:

No

Name *Adele Tivthier* æt 43

Received 23 *mch* 18*9*0 from *Longue Pointe*

Sex *Female* Religion *R.C.* Cause of Death

Buried in the *R. C.* Cemetery on

the 188

REMARKS:

Name *Wm Clugh* æt 45 _

Received *March* 29 18*9*0 from *General Hospital*

Sex *male* Religion *P* Cause of Death

Buried in the *Mount Royal* Cemetery on

the 188

REMARKS:

Name *Rose Bodin* aet 65
Received *April 18* . 1890 *from* Langue Point

Sex female *Religion* R.C *Cause of Death*

Buried in the R C *Cemetery on*

the August 26 189 0

REMARKS:

Name John Shiney aet 58
Received April 18 1890 *from* Hôtel Dieu

Sex male *Religion* R.C *Cause of Death*

Buried in the R.C *Cemetery on*

the 188

REMARKS:

Name *Marcella Langlois* æt 85

Received *April 25* 1890 from *Longue Pointe*

Sex *male* Religion *R.C.* Cause of Death

Buried in the *R.C.* _____ Cemetery on

the _____ 188

REMARKS:

Name *Maxime Pigeon* æt 40

Received *April 26* 1890 from ~~Hôtel Dieu~~ *Longue Pointe*

Sex *male* Religion *R.C.* Cause of Death

Buried in the *R.C.* Cemetery on

the _____ 188

REMARKS:

Name Marie Pinard *aet 56*
    Received May 3 1880 *from* Lague Pointe
Sex female *Religion* R.C. , *Cause of Death*
Buried in the   R.C.   *Cemetery on*
the   188

REMARKS:

Name Leontine Frizelle *aet 27*
    Received May 3 1880 *from* Lague Pointe
Sex female *Religion* RC *Cause of Death*
Buried in the   RC   *Cemetery on*
the   188

REMARKS:

Name *Jacques Proulx* act 66
    Received May 5 1890 from *Lingue Pointe*
Sex male Religion R.C. *Cause of Death*
Buried in the R.C. *Cemetery on*
the 188

REMARKS:

Name *Kenneth Scovie*
    Received May 13 1890 from *Lingue Pointe*
Sex female Religion R.C. *Cause of Death*
Buried in the R.C. *Cemetery on*
the 188

REMARKS:

REMARKS:

Name Victoria Thibault
Received May 15 1890 *from* Longue Pointe
Sex female *Religion* R.C. *Cause of Death*
Buried in the R.C. *Cemetery on*
the 188

REMARKS:

Name Joseph St Pierre
Received May 15 1890 *from* Longue Pointe
Sex male *Religion* R.C. *Cause of Death*
Buried in the R.C. *Cemetery on*
the 188

REMARKS:

Name *George Hart* . act 60

Received May 24 1890 from *Hotel Dieu*

Sex *male* Religion *R.C.* , Cause of Death

Buried in the .... *R.C.* , ... Cemetery on

the _____ 188 _____

REMARKS:

Name *Leon Paillé* act 57

Received May 16 1896 from *Longue Pointe*

Sex *male* Religion *R.C.* , Cause of Death

Buried in the .... *R.C.* , Cemetery on

the 188

REMARKS:

Name John Roone aet 42
  Received May 21° 1880 *from* Lacque Pointe
Sex male *Religion* P *Cause of Death*
Buried in the Mount Royal *Cemetery on*
the 188

REMARKS:

Name Michael Doyle aet 35
  Received May 20² 188 *from* Hôtel Dieu
Sex male *Religion* R.C. *Cause of Death* R.C.
Buried in the *Cemetery on*
the 188

REMARKS:

Name *Alex. Demnais*

Received *May 26* 18?0 *from* *Montreal* Jail

Sex male *Religion* R.C. Cause of Death

Buried in the R.C. Cemetery on

the 188

REMARKS:

Name Ozarie Leblanc oct. 36

Received May 27 18?0 *from* Longue Pointe

Sex male *Religion* R.C. Cause of Death

Buried in the R.C. Cemetery on

the 188

REMARKS:

Name *Jean Baptiste Poirier. aet 50*
  Received *Sept 30 — 1890* from *Hotel Dieu*
Sex *male* Religion *R.C.* Cause of Death *aneurism*
Buried in the *R.C.* Cemetery on
the 188

Name *Alfred Lagrum aet 72*
  Received *Sept 30* 1890 from *Hotel Dieu*
Sex *male* Religion *R.C.* Cause of Death *Septicaemia*
Buried in the *R.C.* Cemetery on
the 188

Name *James* *Moran* – 16

Received *November* 24 18*9*0 from *N. G. H.*

Sex *male* Religion *RC* Cause of Death *Typhoid fever*

Buried in the *RC*. Cemetery on

the   188

REMARKS:

Name *Margaret Canning* – 35 –

Received *Dec* 12 18*9*0 from *Hotel Dieu*

Sex *female* Religion *RC* Cause of Death *Phthisis*

Buried in the *RC*. Cemetery on

the   188

REMARKS:

Name *Francis Kane* ael 50   115

  Received Dec 22ᵈ 1890 *from* Hôtel Dieu

Sex   *Religion* R.C., *Cause of Death* Eczema(?)

Buried in the   RC

the   188   *Cemetery on*

REMARKS:

Name John Burton ael 50

  Received December 31 1890 *from* Hôtel Dieu

Sex male *Religion* R.C., *Cause of Death* Phthisis

Buried in the   RC

the   188   *Cemetery on*

REMARKS:

Name Napoleon Savarie ael 27

  Received January 3ᵈ 1891 *from* Longue Pointe

Sex male *Religion* R.C., *Cause of Death* Marasmus ?

Buried in the   RC

the   188   *Cemetery on*

REMARKS:

Name *Myra Ann Goff* æt 50   116

    Received *January 21ˢᵗ* 1891 *from* *Longue Pointe*

Sex *female* Religion *P -*   *Cause of Death* *General Debility*

Buried in the *Mount Royal*   Cemetery on

the   188

REMARKS:

Name *William Hodge* æt 22

    Received *January 22* 1891 *from* *Longue Point*

Sex *male* Religion *P*   *Cause of Death* *Phthisis*

Buried in the *Mount Royal*   Cemetery on

the   188

REMARKS:

Name *Alexander Gallinger* æt 50

    Received *February 5ᵗʰ* 1891 *from* *Longue Pointe*

Sex *male* Religion *R.C.* *Cause of Death* *Anæmia Epilepsy*

Buried in the *R.C.*   Cemetery on

the   188

REMARKS:

Name Mary Day 50
  Received Feby 11 1891 *from* M.G.H
Sex female *Religion* RC *Cause of Death* Morb Cardia
Buried in the _____ RC *Cemetery on*
the _____ 188___

REMARKS:

Name Victorine Marechal aet 39 Pthisis
  Received February 14 1891 *from* Longue Pointe Asylm
Sex female *Religion* RC *Cause of Death* Pthisis
Buried in the RC *Cemetery on*
the ___ 188___

REMARKS:

Name *Philomene St. Jean* aet 15
Received *March 9* 1891 from *Bon Pasteur*
Sex *female* Religion *R.C.*, Cause of Death *paralysis of brain (?)*
Buried in the   Cemetery on
the   188
REMARKS:

Name *Lilian Nicholson* aet 21
Received *March 11* 1891 from *Maternité (St. Pelagie)*
Sex *female* Religion *R.C.* Cause of Death *Consumption*
Buried in the   Cemetery on
the   188
REMARKS:

Name *Casimir Guerin* aet 60   119

Received *March 16* 1891 *from* Hôtel Dieu

Sex *Male* Religion *R.C.* Cause of Death *Bronchitis*

Buried in the   Cemetery on

the   188

REMARKS:

Name *Antoine Renaud* aet 80

Received *March 21* 1891 *from* Notre Dame Hospital

Sex *Male* Religion *R.C.* Cause of Death *Debility*

Buried in the   Cemetery on

the   188

REMARKS:

Name *Adolphe Blondeau* aet 57

Received *March 26* 1891 *from* Longue Pointe

Sex *male* Religion *R.C.* Cause of Death *Paralysis*

Buried in the   Cemetery on

the   188

REMARKS:

1884 – 1885.

Statement of the Receipts and Expenditure of the Dissecting b
of McGill College from April 1st 1884 to April 1st 1885

Receipts

April 1st 1884.	Balance in C.D. & Bank	$81.36
June 26 "	For two bodies used in Summer Session	28.00
Oct. 3 "	Students fees	205.00
Oct. 18 "	" "	405.00
" "	Balance of Summer Session Grant of $87.00 for Anatomical Purposes after sending $38.60 to Weiss for instruments	48.20
Dec 20th		50.00
	Annual interest on deposit	4.25
March 24th 1885	Students fee	5.00
" " "	Dr Shepherds subjects	26.00
		852.81

1884 – 1885.

Statement of Expenditure

The purchase of subjects from April 1st 1884
to April 1st 1885.

Forty one subjects — $ 381.00

Other Expenditure

Oct 3.	Hire for dissecting room _	$48.45
7.	Chemicals	50.00
11	Tallow.	5.00
10.	Removal of subjects	50.00
28.	Carpenter	6.84
29.	Printing & Stationery	6.07
30	Stools for dissecting room	4.00
21.	Rams	2.40
Nov 25.	Chemicals	30.00
Jan 16.	Improving gas lights	3.07
23	Chemicals	57.45
Feb 20.	Purchase of Bone preparation	3.50

~~233 08~~

$ 614.08

Total per 1884 – 1885.

Total Receipts $ 852.81
Expenditure   614.08
Balance in CDS. Bank   238.73.

1885 — 1886

Statement from April 1st 1885 – April 1st 1886.

Receipts

April 1. 1885. Balance in CDS Bank.	$238.73
Aug 3. 1885. From Summer Session Subjects —	26.00
Oct 1st 1885 Students fees	500.00
Dec. 31st Interest.	5.20
Apr. 29th Money returned after purchase of Anatomical Syringe &c.	9.25
	$779.18

Expenditure

Petty Disbursements.	17.81
Apr 6. Undertakers account in part	100.00
Oct 15. 2 allow	2.50
Oct 15. Medical Hall a/c for Drugs	75.25
Nov 19th 85. Saws & gas stove	5.58
Feb 11th 86 Skeleton	26.50
Feb 18. " Chalks	1.50
Registry of Deaths in Trinity Church	7.00
Mar 23rd Do Bailey for Osteology	4.00
Purchase of 44. Subjects	436.00
	676.14

Total Receipts.	779.18
Expenditure	676.14
Balance CDS. Bank	163.04

1886 – 1887

Receipts

April 1st/886

    Balance in C D S Bank   .03.54

Apr 7-86 –   Students fees   160.50

May 14. 86 – Three bodies paid for by Wilkens. 39.00

Oct 13th '86 Students fees   500.00

Nov 25th 86 Money returned by friends   12.00
          for a subject

Oct 29th   Students fees   70.00

Dec 31   Interest on Deposit   6.10

                          $ 890.14

Expenditure

Purchase of 42 subjects – $ 406.00

Drugs - principally alcohol   127.10

Gordon & Egan for two small trucks 23.54

Undertakers account in part   39.00

Petty Expenditure —   9.89

      Boiler   2.50

      Painting   10.50

      Bone Cleaning   4.00

                      675.03

          Total Receipts 890.14
    Total Expenditure 675.03

Balance in C D S Bank $ 215.11

Annual Statement
1887 – 1888.

Receipts

April 1st 1887.

Balance in C & D Savings Bank	$215.11
Students fees	660.00
Summer Session Subjects	26.00
Money returned by friends of claimed bodies	13.00
Annual Interest	6.66
	$920.77

Expenditure

April 1st/87 to April 1st/88.

Purchase of new subjects	$445.00
Tallow	5.92
Bailly for mounting bones & for anatomical model	20.00
Petty disbursements	10.51
Wray for transport of bodies	155.00
Gordon & Egan for lining tank	29.00
Dr Finley's honorarium	50.00
Drugs & Chemicals &c	45.88
A glass case for new anatomical models	40.00
	$801.31.

Total Receipts 920.77
„   Expenditure 801.31/
Balance in Bank $119.46

R H MacDonnell

Sept 30' 1888 –
Oct 1st 1889

1888–89
Receipts

Students fees	$625.00
Operative Surgery	20.00
	$645.00

Expenditure

Inspectors fees for 58 subjects —	579.00
Returned to Mrs Macd. —	30.00
Wray's &c	90.50
Grays &c	23.70
D. Finley	50.00
Tallow – Bone Forceps, Saw &c	15.00
	$788.20

Receipts 645.00
Expenditure 788.20
Deficit $143.20

W. Sutherland
for F.J.S —

1889 - 90

Receipts

		₤
Balance from Dr Mac Dunnell for 1888		6.10
Students fees from Dr Steward	—	705.00
Summer Session fees	—	24.00
Operative Surgery Subjects		20.00
Money Returned by friends	—	15.00
		$ 770.10

Expenditure

1889

Wrays &c to Sept 30th 1889	—	159.00
Grays &c for Chemicals	—	8.80
Dyers &c " "	—	34.55
Tallow	—	8.00
Record books (Simson)		3.75
Inspectors fee for 13 Subjects	—	132.00
Sundries for Dissecting Room	—	10.70
Balance due Dr Sutherland for 1888-9	—	143.20

Dr Sutherland

1890

Inspectors fee for 35 subjects		348.00
Wrays &c from Oct. 3rd 1889 – April 1890		67.00
Boxes & Burials to April 1st 1890		25.50
	$	940.50

35
1/3
4/5

Receipts $ 770.10
Expenditure 940.50
Deficit $ 170.40

www.ingramcontent.com/pod-product-compliance
Lightning Source LLC
Chambersburg PA
CBHW030601270326
41927CB00007B/1001